My Life as a List

198

199

200

201

202

203

204

205

206

My Life as a List

207 THINGS ABOUT MY (BRONX) CHILDHOOD

by Linda Rosenkrantz

CLARKSON POTTER/PUBLISHERS
New York

Published by Clarkson N. Potter, Inc., 201 East 50th Street, New York,
New York 10022. Member of the Crown Publishing Group.

Random House, Inc. New York, Toronto, London, Sydney, Auckland
www.randomhouse.com

CLARKSON N. POTTER, POTTER, and colophon are registered
trademarks of Random House, Inc.

Printed in the United States of America

Design by Marysarah Quinn

Library of Congress Cataloging-in-Publication Data
Rosenkrantz, Linda.
My life as a list : 207 things about my (Bronx)
childhood / by Linda Rosenkrantz.—1st ed.
p.   cm.
1. Rosenkrantz, Linda—Childhood and youth.   2. Jews—New
York (State)—New York—Biography.   3. Bronx (New York,
N.Y.)—Biography.   I. Title.
F128.9.J5R58 1999
974.7′275004924′0092—dc21
[B]   98-27681
                                                 CIP

ISBN 0-609-60367-1

10   9   8   7   6   5   4   3   2   1
FIRST EDITION

My Life as a List

1. Before I was born, my mother had decided to name me either Laurel or Lydia, names that appealed to her artistic temperament. But then somehow, while under the scrim of anesthesia, she was convinced by my father's sisters to make me a lackluster Ruth, in honor of their recently deceased mother, Rose. And so my birth certificate read Ruth Leila, a name I was never ever called, by my mother, either of my father's sisters, or anyone else. Instead, I was known by my Jewish name, variously spelled (and spoken) Leya or Laila.

2. My great-aunt Pauline, youngest of my bubba's sisters, served as my surrogate New York grandmother. For the first seven years of my life, she lived in the apartment right below ours on West Tremont Avenue. There was a dumbwaiter that moved on thick rope pulleys just inside the kitchens of all the apartments in the building for the collection of garbage, and I have the distinct recollection of being sent back and forth (up and down) between Aunt Pauline and Uncle Harry's apartment and ours, tied into the dumbwaiter with a heavy, scratchy cord, but my mother says it must have been a dream. (Do you really think we'd let you sit in a thing where people put their filthy dirty garbage?)

~

3. My mother's skin was as soft and smooth as her pale blue satin nightgown. On Sunday mornings, I would crawl into bed between my parents (leaning more against my mother's pillowy belly) and regale them with such songs as "You Must Have Been a Beautiful Baby."

~

4. My grandfather, strangely enough, also had skin as soft and smooth as satin.

~

5. I would sometimes catch my grandmother gazing adoringly at her two sons in a way in which she never looked at any of her three daughters (but did sometimes look at me).

6. When I started school, Miss Sargoy, my kindergarten teacher, quite naturally looked at my Delaney card and called me Ruth. I had no idea who she was talking to. Arriving home in tears that first day, I was told by my mother that if it would make me feel better I could start from scratch and choose a completely new name. As long as it began with the letter R or L, to match my Jewish name of Razel Leya. She went through a long list of names beginning with R (Renee? Rhoda? Rita? Roberta? Rochelle? Rosalind?) and L (Leah? Lenore? Leonore? Lois? Loretta? Lorraine?). I finally chose Linda because it sounded so much shinier and more modern than all the others (having no way of knowing that in a few years it would become the most popular girl's name in America). In any case, though, I soon discovered that I didn't know who this Linda was any more than I had known who that Ruth was.

NAME *Linda Rosenkrantz*

TRAINING IN PERSONALITY
Desirable Traits

	Oct. 21 Mar. 15	Dec. 15 May 15	Jan. 31 Jun. 20
1. Works and plays well with others.	U S	I S	S S
2. Completes work	U S	I S	S S
3. Is generally careful	S	S	C
4. Respects the rights of others.	S	S	S
5. Practices good health habits.	S	S	S
6. Speaks clearly	B+	A	B+
7. *Conduct*			
8.			

Scholarship

	Oct. 21 Mar. 15	Dec. 15 May 15	Jan. 31 Jun. 20
Reading	A	S	S
Literature	A	S	S
Composition	B+	S	S
Spelling	B+	S	S
Arithmetic			
Geography	B	S	S
History and Civics			
Penmanship			
Health Education			
Art			
Music			
Nature			
Sewing or Construction			

MEANING OF RATINGS

S—Satisfactory   U—Unsatisfactory
I—Improvement is shown
A—Excellent   B—Good
C—Passable   D—Failing

When per cent. ratings are used, ...% is the passing rating, except in Spelling, where ....% is required.

NEEDED IMPROVEMENT

First Period	Second Period	Third Period
		Nice Research Work

7. My mother kept a box of manila folders containing the materials for Nice Research Work. In it were pictures she had cut out from magazines (mostly the *Saturday Evening Post*) filed under such topics as ANIMALS AND BIRDS, FAMOUS PEOPLE, FOREIGN COUNTRIES. Then when I came home for lunch (creamed mushrooms on toast, tomato surprise) and told her my report assignment (screech owls? Peter Minuit?), she could dash to her file and find the appropriate pictures even before I had punctured the skin on my butterscotch pudding. Nice Research Work.

～

8. All my elementary school teachers (the Misses Sargoy, Ferber, Turner, Johnson, Gargan, Delaney—as in the card—Leon and Tartt) had identical handwriting. Two of them (Sargoy, Tartt) were named Cecilia and three of them (Gargan, Leon, Tartt) had hair the color and texture of sun-bleached brick, Miss Leon with a mustache to match. Miss Turner (Class 2B) gave me the only two report card Unsatisfactories (Works and plays well with others, Is generally careful) I ever got, but she did make special note of Nice Research Work.

~

9. I memorized a story called "Abdullah's Onions," which was essentially about the power of bad breath, and, dressed in my pleated navy blue skirt, white middy blouse, and red tie, recited it in the school auditorium at the weekly Assembly.

~

10. Each times table gave off a different aura. The twos, threes, and fours were like playful babies. Five was even-tempered and benign, six beginning to get a bit troublesome (only five fingers on one hand, after all), but it was the sevens and eights and to some extent the nines (which did have some logic to them if you slowed down and stopped panicking for a minute or two) that were impossible brats, under control one day, out of reach the next. Eleven, on the other hand, was an absolute laugh riot, and the twin multiplicands—$6 \times 6, 7 \times 7, 9 \times 9$—had the sweet, rich taste of a chocolate eclair.

11. I had a recurrent dream in which Adolf Hitler, in full high-booted uniform, came to our apartment door and demanded to know if I was Jewish. When I shook my head no, one of his squad of similarly booted Storm Troopers who was searching the premises would always happen upon my Hebrew School book, even though I had stuck it way at the back of the bookcase, and drag me and my parents off.

~

12. I sometimes had the thought that my mother might in fact be a spy for Hitler and so I watched her actions very closely, just waiting for the inevitable moment when she would betray herself. What a perfect cover, I'd think knowingly, a Jewish housewife in the Bronx.

~

13. My grandmother cut a slot into the top of her Serutan (natureS spelled backward) tin and dropped all her spare change into it, saving up to buy me a $25 war bond.

~

14. My mother made little puppets out of peanuts and sewed teeny dresses for them to wear over their shells. They were marionettes, actually, with strings, and we kept them in a cigar box.

~

15. One thing I could never quite fathom was how people were able to recognize me when I was out doing the daily shopping with my mother on the Avenue. How could they possibly tell me apart from every other little (Jewish) girl my age when there was absolutely nothing to distinguish me? Was it just because I was with my mother and therefore had to be her daughter? At least when I reached school age and was sent to Cousin George Hulnick the optometrist and got the

despised (but playing-field–leveling) blue-framed eye-glasses, there was something concrete to set me apart.

~

16. While we were making the daily rounds (ration books in Mommy's purse), my mother would intone her anxious mantra: "What shall I make Daddy for dinner tonight?" In truth, this didn't seem like that difficult a problem to me, since she always served one of the following: lamb chops, breaded veal chops, tenderloin steak (Romanian style), hamburgers (flat and dry), chicken-in-the-pot, liver (flat and dry), franks and beans, or salmon patties. Accompanied by mashed potatoes and a canned (later frozen) vegetable, followed by Libby's fruit cocktail or cling peaches. And preceded (it was ordained, possibly by Fannie Farmer or Emily Post, that there be three courses in every meal) by half a grapefruit liberally sprinkled with sugar, or half a baked eggplant swimming in oil, the latter's pulp a pale green, snotlike color that made me feel slightly iggy. (How can he swallow that stuff?)

17. For me, the worst store on the Avenue was the button store. It looked innocent enough on the outside, not much different in aspect from Dora's Yarn Shop or Moe & Willie's Notion Store. But the interior was the stuff of nightmares: long tall rows of shelves piled high with boxes of buttons, each with a sample sewn to the front, some with two eyes, some with four, all staring, glaring down directly at me.

18. My grandparents bought a seesaw set for me to use on our summer sojourns in Attleboro and installed it in their backyard. But the first time I went up on it the ground below became a myopic blur and so I never rode on it again, feeling the queasiness of failure every time I saw it. At one point the metal started to rust, and when I arrived the following summer it was gone, replaced by a much less threatening (level playing field) croquet set.

19. All my aunts and great-aunts floated but none of them swam. One day at the beach I was told to watch my great-aunt Annie (never quite the same after her minor stroke), but I'd left my glasses on the blanket and it wasn't till she was drifting off to sea that I noticed she was out of sight, I didn't know where, halfway back to the Old Country, and I had to fetch someone else to swim out and bring her back.

20. My father never learned to swim or drive. At one point, he did take some driving lessons, but when he went for the test, he became annoyed at the inspector for arriving five minutes late, told him so in no uncertain terms, and that was the end of that.

21. I thought it was really rude when people described my hair color as dirty blond. Or when they asked me why I looked so sad when I wasn't.

∼

22. My grandparents' around-the-corner Massachusetts neighbors, Francisco Raymundo, a sandal-wearing Filipino artist, and his wife, Ruth Adams (of the Quincy Adams Adamses and an ex-schoolmate of my mother's) Raymundo, offered me my first taste of pork, a hitherto forbidden fruit. I thought I had never tasted anything so sweet and delicious in my life.

∼

23. Francisco Raymundo called me "petal face" and "flower face" and did a portrait of me in pastels when I was four. The delineation of the face was fine and delicate (petal, flower) but he made the hands Siqueiros-big and square, saying that ultimately what power I would have would come from those hands. He sent my mother a letter ("Dear Leya's mother") with precise framing instructions ("As Leya is face down on glazed paper, apply paper hanger's paste on Leya's back").

∼

24. I was excited to get letters from his daughter Abbie Raymundo, who was two and a half years older than I and who addressed me variously (once we passed out of the Leya phase) as Linda, Lin Lin, Wong-Wong, or Right Honorable Wong-Wong Lee Fong, and herself as Scotty (because she prided herself on being cheap),

I HOPE. I earnestly hope!

        _ personally, too, I only give the dimensions of frame to picture framers and make the frame for me. I DO NOT , AT ANY TIME, LEAVE PASTEL PORTRAIT WITH FRAMERS. Pastel portraits <u>are not</u> oil paintings and NEVER WILL BE!

        _ your frame should either have a thick mat (beveled) or an invisible buffer - so pastel portrait will not come in contact with glass.

        _ I could have mounted Leya myself, but your folks did not give me time to do it. They were in a hurry, very much in a hurry - oh, very much so.

        _ thank you.

        The mounting board should be perfectly smooth. If it is rough and <u>indenty</u> - and <u>holey</u>; they(the indentations and holes) will show in Leya's face and arms. . . . like chicken pox and small pox - and leprosy. Bah!

        _ well, dasall, my dear; glad to know Sam likes LeYa's.

    IN CASE OF DOUBT WITH REGARD TO MOUNTING, GET IN TOUCH WITH ME. _ with a bow of devotion to Leya's sweet, little flower face

                        _ always sincerely

ABBIE RAYMUNDO
50 HOLMAN ST.
ATTLEBORO, MASS.
2/8/44

Dear W. W. L. F.,

I have decoded your message. I am replying. The key to my code is to be found in the envelope.

DRKG HYILB GY ROIO KLYFG BYFI MYFHIX. SH RSH XKWB? DKH SG PKGKV?

Plenty has happened since you left. At school I've had practically all the A demerits obtainable. So've been relieved of all my special duties, and teacher investigates every move I make. I hear the 3rd degree about every day. I'm in dutch with all the teachers. Luckily I was no where on the premises at the time $1.18 was stolen from the lunch counter at school. At my school our room is having a play about Washington. I'm the Mistress of Ceremonies. Are you giving any valentines this year? I'm not. Don't you ever get into trouble at school?

Snippy (also the name of her dog), "Pistol Packin'" Abbie, Detective Inspector Abbie, CX4, and The Right Honorable Abbie Raymundo, Ambassadress Extraordinary Plenipotentiary. In black ink, green ink, and white ink on blue paper, in mirror writing and on handcrafted jigsaw puzzle pieces, she regaled me with tales of trips to the cemetery and the junk yard, of bringing dead snakes to school, climbing trees and thirty-foot water towers, playing hooky ("Don't you *ever* get in trouble in school?"), her nefarious black-market activities, and knocking out the tooth of a girl named Derythe Cleggs in a fight, all of which made small-town New England life seem a lot more interesting and exotic than that of the big city.

~

25. Once my mother opened a bar of (Hershey's? Nestlé's?) milk chocolate and it was crawling with ants.

~

26. When I learned that George Rabinowitz, a rumpled, wavy-black-haired boy in my class (white shirt always pulling out of his pants) who reminded me somewhat of my rumpled, wavy-black-haired father, had died of polio over the summer, I couldn't believe it. I immediately wrote a poem beginning with the lines, "They told me George Rabinowitz was dead and I didn't understand what they meant by dead." And for the next couple of years, when I woke up in the morning the first thing I did was raise my legs, one at a time, checking for any signs of stiffness or pain, terrified that the raging epidemic might have infiltrated my room during the night.

~

27. One day I decided to test my endurance for pain. Sitting on my bed in my underpants, I rhythmically, stoically scratched back and forth across a half-inch strip of my waistline, until the gash was deep and bleeding, leaving a permanent scar.

28. I liked getting scabs on my knees when I fell while roller skating because it made me feel regular. I liked anything that made me feel regular.

~

29. My mother's friend Rose Schwartz, who often called me Lizzie Tish, whizzed through (my) life like a dynamo, zooming off to work every day and leaving her overburdened daughter Margery (my designated best  friend) to rush her little brother over to her bubba Taitel's (whose mean-spirited husband was known universally as Simon Legree) after school in a bulky black stroller laden with bags of laundry, so that Margery could then dash off to her Hebrew and piano lessons. Whew. I found it a breathless struggle to keep up with her. ("Why can't you be more like Margery? What do *you* do to help *your* mother?")

~

30. Margery had such a busy schedule, she had to wear a watch.

so busy she had to wear a watch

31. At Camp Jekoce, the Jewish Community Center of Poughkeepsie camp Margery Schwartz and I were sent to along with my Poughkeepsie cousin Naomi, I spent a good deal of my time hiding under the bed. I also managed to contract mild (but just serious enough to be sent home) cases of pneumonia two summers in a row.

~

32. At dancing school, I refused to move off the mat.

15

33. At my Parsons School of Design Saturday art class, I painted nothing but girls in Cinderella-ish (Mother's nightgown) pale blue ball gowns. I loved mixing that blue tempera paint with large amounts of white, stopping just at the point when it was about to lose any sense of blueness.

~

34. When I was four, I was deeply humiliated when I went into the hospital to have my tonsils removed and they put me in a crib. A crib!

35. When I was seven, I was deeply humiliated when my uncle Al and his then wife Mildred (Mickey), the first of his three *shiksa* wives, brought me a Pinocchio pull toy. A pull toy!

~

36. When I was very young I called my mother "Pinocchio nose" and drew profiles of her in the air featuring a huge schnozz and a curlicue mass of double/triple chins.

~

37. I joined the Danny Kaye Fan Club (he reminded me slightly of my sandy-haired Uncle Sam) and got mimeographed copies of *Kaye's Kapers* in the mail. I also wrote letters to Van Johnson and Peter Lawford, c/o Metro-Goldwyn-Mayer Studios, Culver City, California.

~

38. I automatically hated anyone who came from Brooklyn. Except Danny Kaye.

39. I took a certain pride in the existence of the definite article in front of the word Bronx, as if it elevated my borough (far above Brooklyn, needless to say) to the position of a grand duchy or some distant continental locale, like The Hague or The Netherlands, The World, The Universe.

~

40. I had about twenty pen pals from all over the country plus one in South America, Aida, the niece of my mother's old Attleboro (heavyset spinster) friend Elsie DeCastro. The others came from such equally mysterious places as Shelby, Ohio, and Davenport, Iowa. I wrote to them about my hobbies and activities, the books I was reading, and my favorite movie stars, and they wrote back about their siblings and pets and their favorite movie stars. Most of them found it hard to conceive of a child, a family, actually living in New York City.

~

41. I would anxiously await the arrival of Smitty the mailman, who came whistling into the building twice a day, morning and afternoon. I'd listen for the jingle of his keys, then the sound of the master key opening the lock of the top tier of brass boxes, and run down the stairs to greet him, hoping perhaps for a V-Mail message from Uncle Al or Eddie, a letter from one of my pen pals, or an autographed photo of Peter Lawford.

~

42. Abbie Raymundo sent me a copy of her self-authored, handwritten booklet "How to Burp," giving numerous multicultural (e.g., the Chinese After Tea Burp) variations on the theme. After extensive, if alienating, practice, I became a pretty fair master of the art myself.

~

43. Seeing Hedy Lamarr's ravishingly beautiful face fill the screen in the movie *Tortilla Flat* one Saturday afternoon at the Park Plaza Theater gave me something approaching my first orgasm.

~

44. For the most part, my favorites of the girl stars were the impossibly sweet ones (no, not June Allyson): Jeanne Crain, Joan Caulfield, Joan Leslie.

~

45. My favorite picture book was *The Wise Old Aardvark*, the story of a wiseman-turned-anteater who got a job giving diabolically clever solutions over the radio to the perplexing problems of people all over the world—such as a Chinese family whose grandmother had been carried up into the sky by a huge balloon, some Eskimos who saw two scary eyes glaring out of their igloo, and two Egyptians whose camels hated each other. The wise old aardvark finally earned enough money to retire and employ an esteemed Italian singer named Signor Pompinelli Ragusa to sing to him exclusively for the rest of his life.

46. When I was too young to navigate the heavily trafficked (cars, trolleys, trucks) street separating my apartment house from my school, I would approach a stranger and say "Can you cross me?" following my mother's daily charge: "Be sure to ask someone to cross you." No one ever refused. I would often look up and see Aunt Pauline at her window, watching to see that I was all right.

with Aunt Pauline

47. There were four external constants in my childhood: the Mayor (Fiorello H. La Guardia), the Governor (Thomas E. Dewey), the President (Franklin Delano Roosevelt), and the War.

48. At a certain moment in time, a large number of the little Jewish girls in the West Bronx whose apartments were too small to house a piano suddenly began taking accordion lessons, struggling through such Latinate favorites as "Come Back to Sorrento" and "O Sole Mio." I was one of that ragtag band, practicing (standing up facing the music stand) and feeling foolish in front of our large ground-floor living-room window in full view of all the neighborhood kids (why didn't I move farther back out of sight?) as they skated by or played stickball in the street. Each time I hit a wrong note, my mother would call out "C-sharp!" or "E-flat!" from the kitchen, where she was breading the veal chops or shaping the salmon patties. Her pitch—like so many other things about her—was perfect. (My mother wanted everything in the world to be perfect, penciling in long, beautiful lashes on the eyes of all the women in our family snapshots.)

49. My accordion teacher's name was Mark Friedman. He was a sad-eyed, tawny-haired man in his early thirties who wore glasses and whose legs and lower torso had been paralyzed by polio. He shared a small, dark, garlicky apartment about five blocks from mine with his dark, heavy-lidded mother, and each moment I was with him I felt the leaden weight of his ironic burden, that of spending his days trying to teach tone-deaf little Jewish girls how to play "Come Back to Sorrento" on the accordion. Every few weeks, for a little light relief, he would assign me a handwritten copy of a currently popular tune like "Don't Fence Me In" or "Mairzy Doats" and if I played it so that it was at least minimally recognizable, he would reward me by playing something on the piano, a thrilling piece by Chopin or Gershwin—almost the only time (see number 50) I ever saw the bitterness temporarily wane.

POSTAL SAVINGS PLAN

for the Purchase of

UNITED STATES

DEFENSE

SAVINGS BONDS

$1 STAMPS

$100 BONDS

50. My aunt Beck offered to buy me a $25 war bond if I could master "The Flight of the Bumble Bee," à la Harry James, a challenge so ludicrous that it even brought a smile to Mark Friedman's face.

51. I was in the middle of my regular 4:30 Thursday accordion lesson one April afternoon when Mark Friedman's mother burst into the room saying over and over, "President Roosevelt is dead! President Roosevelt is dead!" Mark Friedman put his head against the piano and began to weep, and I was so stunned that I couldn't even enjoy the relief of having my lesson cut short.

52. If I waited (stalled) long enough, Mommy would do it for me.

53. If I couldn't find the words, Mommy would say them for me.

~

54. I couldn't fathom how a piano-playing haberdasher named Harry could presume to step into the shoes of the godlike Franklin Delano Roosevelt. Partly because my uncle Harry was a haberdasher and he would never have been able to handle such a big job.

55. When I was in kindergarten, boys still had names like Bertram, Marvin, Sheldon, Harold, Jerome, and Eugene. The girls were Elaine and Eileen, Joyce and Jeanette, Lita and Anita, and the twins, Arlene and Nadine.

56. Among my fellow students in my first-grade class at P.S. 104 were a pair of twins; a boy named Harold, whose mouth looked as though it had been carved (Charlie McCarthy–like) from wood; a girl named Dorothy, who limped; a girl named Lita, who had a big head and who talked too much; a girl named Gladys, whose father may or may not have been in prison; a girl named Gail Pritzger, who looked and moved like a delicate black-eyed ballerina; and a girl named Joyce, who once threw up inside the clothing closet and whose name (for me) carried the stench of vomit forever after.

~

57. When I was in the fifth grade (not "when I was in fifth grade," as it is said everywhere but New York City), we had for a few years been split into classes arranged according to academic status. The highest was 5-1-1, followed by 5-1-3, 5-1-4, 5-1-5, 5-1-6, and finally (who did they think they were kidding?), the lowest of the low, 5-1-2. At one point the crème de la crème of the 5-1-1 girls decided that each of us would select one of the crème de la crème of the 6-1-1 boys to become the object of our passionate devotion and discussion, prank phone calls, and anonymous notes. Carole (the final "e" had been added to her name just that year) Siskind chose Ira Potashner and demanded to be addressed as Mrs. Potashner. Marlene Levine zeroed in on Bobby Berliner. And I picked Alan Arman, a short blond boy whom I had liked since the day he pulled the belt off my (scratchy) woolen snowsuit while chasing me around the playground several years earlier.

58. While the Alans, Iras, and Bobbys studiously ignored us, there was another group of boys with a different agenda entirely. They developed a practice referred to as "jumping," which we nonchalantly accepted as a matter of course. Simply stated, as we walked home from school, arithmetic and spelling books dangling from a strap, they jumped on our backs and threw us to the ground, after which we blithely picked ourselves up and kept walking. One day, a boy named Harvey Gerringer (6-1-6), who lived at the far end of my block, jumped me as usual, but instead of going straight down, I happened to fall into a lamppost. My glasses broke and blood and shattered shards were everywhere. My faithful friend Sulamith (Sunny) Berman cautiously led me home only to find that my mother and Aunt Pauline had gone downtown to restock their supply of half-size housedresses at Klein's, leaving my in-over-her-head, non-English-speaking, visiting Massachusetts grandmother on after-school-snack duty. In shock, she somehow managed to rush me to the office of Dr. Kavee (a shorter version of Governor Dewey) on the Grand Concourse and the appropriate stitches were taken. (Scar #2.) From then on, the incident was referred to as "So close—thank God it wasn't her eye."

~

59. Marlene Levine and I bought each other matching silver pins in the form of a fork and a spoon and called each other Nip and Sip for a couple of months. Myrna (who preferred to be called Anne) Newman and I referred to each other as "my other half." In fact, her pretty, much older sister Gloria, who was a gym teacher-in-training in our school, addressed her salutations to me in my autograph album as "my sister's other half."

~

60. Barbara Kubrick was so in love with Al Jolson that she insisted on being called Jolie.

~

61. Rose Schwartz made Margery and me drink tepid milk with a raw egg beaten into it, then added insult to injury by calling it a malted. I did my best to dribble it down the sink when she was out of the room. Margery seemed to take it in stride.

~

62. Margery Schwartz's bedroom, at the end of a long, narrow hallway, with my mother's giant painting of Jack and Jill falling down the hill dominating the wall, was excruciatingly neat. Her puzzles and games, stacked on shelves in strict size-place order, were not to be played with, nor was the untouchable dimple-faced Shirley Temple doll with untouchable (dirty) blond ringlets and untouchable red and white polka-dot dress, which always sat on the same spot atop the brown and green plaid bedspread. (There was nothing pink or pastel about Margery's upbringing.)

~

63. While the rest of us were still drawing no-necked girls with banana bunches of fingers, Sulamith (called

Sunny by most people, Salami by some of the meaner boys) Berman was sketching accomplished portraits of chiseled-faced men, a talent that allowed her to form a bond with my nursery rhyme-painting mother. Sunny (wearing white shirts that smelled of starch, the first to sport a sleeveless blouse) called for me every morning before school, and would stand leaning against the refrigerator, waiting for me to finish my last inch of milk (not as tepid as Rose Schwartz's but never quite cold enough) even if she knew it would make her late for school, talking, in a deep, almost masculine, monotone voice, to my mother, mostly about how much she loved to draw, my mother responding in her most encouraging tone. Then we would run the five or six blocks down Nelson Avenue, sometimes getting sharp stitches in our sides, really speeding up once we were across Featherbed Lane, and when we got to the schoolyard on Shakespeare Avenue, she (ragged-edged little red blotches on her cheeks) would have to go to the late line while some of my friends always managed to sneak me into the regular, on-time one.

64. I would sometimes be embarrassed to walk to school with Sunny Berman because she still had her long black braids at least two years after everyone else had cut off theirs.

~

65. In addition to her colossal nursery rhyme canvases, my mother had also in earlier days painted accomplished watercolor replicas of Japanese prints (waves lapping) and *Godey's Lady's Book* fashion plates of stylish Victorian gentlewomen, examples of which could be found in the homes of Rose Schwartz, Aunt Pauline, and others, along with their Metropolitan Museum of Art Masterpiece reproductions of Van Gogh and Vermeer.

~

66. I loved reading dog stories like *Lad: A Dog* and *Heart of a Dog* by Albert Payson Terhune and *Lassie Come-Home* by Eric Knight. I kept a scrapbook of dog pictures (Nice Research Work) and would gaze lovingly into the soulful eyes of the collies and cocker spaniels. I learned the names of all the breeds. I collected little china figurines of Irish setters and Scotties and beagles and bloodhounds and Boston bulls and St. Bernards and poodles and Great Danes and dachshunds and Dalmatians. But let a real dog approach me, large or small, and my feet would freeze in fear.

~

67. None of my friends had dogs (cats were unheard of, turtles and goldfish being the most common ephemeral pets of choice). In fact the only dog I knew personally, aside from Abbie Raymundo's summertime terrier Snippy, was the huge snarling chow, Buddy, who belonged to our snarling super, a big bruiser, truck driver of a woman named Millie, the only bleached blond on the block. Millie lived alone in the basement of our building, surrounded by a graveyard of stored sleds and outgrown tricycles, ornately carved walnut credenzas and tattered Morris chairs, and came out and glared at us if we were making too much noise playing potsy in the alley.

68. My father's youngest sister was only fourteen when she was orphaned and so, when my parents married two years later, Pearl came to live with them. It was not a particularly comfortable situation for any of the principal players and it became even more difficult when I was born and Pearlie had to give up her tiny bedroom and move into the foyer (pronounced foyuh). Pearl despised my mother and all her persnickety New England airs. One day, as I was later told, my mother was walking past my room when she heard the girl crooning quietly beside my crib, "You have a *bad* mother, you have a *good* aunt, you have a *bad* mother, you have a *good* aunt." Within a week, Pearl was gone, shipped off to live (after a miserable short stay with my grandparents in Attleboro) with her two older sisters on Orchard Street.

~

69. Aunt Pearl married Herbie Victor (*hey, that's Victor Herbert in reverse!*), an orphan like his bride, a good-looking, broad-shouldered man in the manner of Brian Donlevy without the mustache. A crooner like his bride, Uncle Herbie liked to sing songs like, "I'm going to buy a paper doll that I can call my own" (which I somehow construed to refer to me), and we (he) hatched a plan by which he would audition for Arthur Godfrey's *Talent Scouts* (Ted Mack's *Amateur Hour?* Major Bowes?) with me accompanying him on the accordion.

~

70. While all my friends couldn't wait to grow up, I couldn't wait to grow old. Well maybe not old exactly, more middle-aged. Just old enough (in those pre-fitness-conscious days) not to be expected to run, swim, jump, climb, hit a ball, ride a bike, or hike. I wanted to sit on the sidelines of the ball with Binnie Barnes, Beulah Bondi, and all those other movie doyennes of a certain age, half hidden behind a fan, gossiping as I watched the young people dance.

71. I worried a lot about how I would manage to walk down the aisle at my wedding without wearing my glasses.

72. I also worried about waltzing with my father at my wedding, both of us being such klutzy dancers.

73. Once, when I had overplayed my hand in trying to avoid going to bed (singing, dancing, "Abdullah's Onions," whatever it took), I overheard my uncle Herbie refer to me as a brat. This definitely went a long way toward diluting my desire to be his accompanist on Arthur Godfrey's *Talent Scouts*.

74. When I was seven, my aunt Helen gave birth to her first baby, which meant I was no longer the only grandchild. I could almost feel the chill of the single-focus spotlight moving off of me.

75. While all around her other mothers were hollering commands, critiques, and (especially) threats at their kids out the window, pinching and pulling their arms, giving them whacks on this or that part of their bodies, mine resolutely held to her belief in the powers of reason and gentle persuasion, rarely raising her voice.

76. Margery Schwartz and I became members of the Junior National Board of Review and went to screenings of movies like *Miss Susie Slagle's* and *The Life and Death of Colonel Blimp* and then wrote down our considered opinions of them and whether or not we would recommend them for other young people. When I was selected to represent the Board on a Dorothy Gordon *New York Times* radio forum addressing the impact of films on the youth of America, my brain, mouth, and tongue froze and all the family gathered around their radios to listen never heard the sound of my voice.

⌒

77. My father's newspaper of choice was the *World Telegram,* later the *World Telegram & Sun,* with an occasional foray into the *Post.* He read his paper during dinner, following the baseball scores (although he really only cared about the Yanks) and racetrack results, and tented it over his face when he stretched out on the couch and fell asleep right after supper. (Shh, Daddy's tired, he works hard all day.)

⌒

78. *The Bronx Home News* was delivered to our apartment door. One day we opened it to find the headline, BRONX GIRL STARTS DRIVE FOR CLOTHING AT THEATRE, over an article proclaiming that "Linda Rosenkrantz, 10, was the first Stanley Theatre patron to donate an article of children's clothing in the Russian Relief Campaign to aid the children of the U.S.S.R. . . . After seeing child actors Vitya Vinogradov, Alik Letichevsky, and Vovo

Ponomariov under the brutal Germans, Linda presented the theatre's director, David Fine, with her brand new woolen muffler with a request that it be sent to Russia." A great to-do was made over me the next day at school, praising my beneficence and the glory it brought to my borough. But the fact of the matter was that this act of altruism had never taken place. I had never even seen Vitya, Vovo, or Alik. My cousin Dave Fine, owner of the Stanley Theatre (which showed Russian films exclusively, a fact that would later cause many a raised eyebrow), had made up the whole story for publicity.

~

79. Every Halloween my costume consisted of wooden clogs, a peasant dress with a white organdy apron over it, and a white Dutch-girl cap with thick yellow yarn pigtails attached.

~

80. I went from bob to braids (sometimes worn Slavic-style on the top of my head) to frizzy preteen perms under the supervision of my mother's beauty parlor man, Sam, who wore a gray smock and looked more like an optician than a beautician. His permanent wave machine was a primitive instrument of torture, singeing the ends of my hair and searing my scalp, and there was scarcely a time that I didn't leave Sam's Beauty Salon in tears. (Why did Margery have to get the naturally curly hair?)

81. When my grandmother and her four sisters got together, they would laugh until tears ran down their cheeks, grimacing as if they were in extreme agony. (There was a sixth sister somewhere whose name was never spoken.) Besides Bubba and the sister whose name was never spoken, Aunt Pauline and Aunt Annie, there was the one sometimes called Rose and sometimes called Rachel, a sweet-tempered seamstress whose brilliant inventor husband was put away into an asylum after he ran through the streets of Providence proclaiming the merits of his rubber-repairing process, and the next-to-youngest, Celia, who was transformed into a bitter woman when her father forced her to marry Morris, the older, almost-illiterate, cigar-chomping vegetable peddler (horse-drawn cart) although she tearfully pleaded with him for days not to.

82. Aunt Pauline, the baby of the family, liked to read thick novels like *War and Peace* and *Anthony Adverse*. Then she would relate the stories to my mother, who was too busy to read, in remarkably precise detail. (As a girl she had researched and written all her favorite brother's debating speeches, for which he received considerable acclaim.) Aunt Pauline was the extended family's arbiter of right and wrong. She could/would have been

played on screen by Maria Ouspenskaya.

83. When Aunt Pauline smiled, I felt that it was a hard-earned reward.

~

84. Aunt Pauline told me that when her father, my great-grandfather, first moved to Attleboro and walked through the streets in his long red, then white beard (God?) and yarmulke, people would throw stones at him. They had never seen a Jew before.

~

85. One of my favorite pastimes was picking the yellow paint off Ti-Con-Der-Oga pencils. (In fact, I derived great satisfaction from picking in general. Nose, toes, ears, belly button, and most particularly the "sleepers" crusting at the corners of my eyes.) In our house we used pencils for everything but signing report cards, checks, insurance policies, and leases.

~

86. I liked to lick almost as much as I liked to pick. I liked to lick my shoulder after a salt-water splash, I liked to lick envelopes and stamps, I liked to lick dripping vanilla Mel-O-Rolls and pistachio sugar cones, and I especially liked to lick the waxy protective paper on the inside of Dixie Cup covers, gradually removing enough ice cream to reveal the circular movie star portrait underneath. (Bing Crosby? Alice Faye? Gloria Jean?)

~

87. There was a dour-looking man named Mr. Katz who came to our apartment door a couple of times a year. After drinking a cup of tea, he would open his valise and from his neatly folded stock my mother would select her season's supply of aprons, dish towels, tablecloths, and napkins. She would never buy these items anywhere else, not from Moe & Willie's Notion Store on the Avenue or even Aunt Jessie's dry goods store in Attleboro.

~

88. When we moved to our new apartment on Brandt Place, one of the first things we noticed was that our next-door neighbors, the Kellers, had a subscription to *The Daily Worker*. Aside from that, they seemed perfectly normal. But it meant that now I had to do double duty, keeping an eye on them, as well as my mother, for possible espionage activity.

~

89. My father's cousin Joe, a jolly version of Edward G. Robinson with a deep cleft in his chin, worked for the John Hancock Life Insurance Company, and every time he came to visit he'd bring me a couple of the instructional pamphlets the company distributed. They ranged from "Samuel Adams, Father of American

Independence" to "Sleep, the Restorer." (Nice Research Work.) By the time Cousin Joe dropped dead at the shocking age of 36, I had a collection of at least 40 John Hancock booklets.

~

90. When my composition on safety won third prize in a city-wide contest, I was called up to the front of the auditorium (white middy blouse) and given a certificate to commemorate my achievement. My essay opened with a dramatic image of people dashing recklessly in front of and between speeding cars in slapstick movies, followed by my admonition that in real life there is no director on the scene to yell "Cut!" Some weeks later I was going through my John Hancock pamphlet collection. As I glanced at the one on safety, I was confronted by—oh no!—that same dramatic image. My body temperature shot up as I was instantly subsumed by shame and guilt. What should I do? Should I tell anyone about it? Should I write a letter to Mayor La

Guardia confessing to this unintentional plagiarism and return the undeserved certificate?

~

91. For every birthday and every Hanukkah, my aunt Helen sent me a big, beautiful illustrated book, with some title like *Myths Every Child Should Know, Tales from Shakespeare, Children of Many Lands,* and *Fairyland of Opera,* not to mention *The Rhyming Dictionary & Poet's Handbook* (yet more Nice Research Work), all inscribed in the flowery, flowing hand that I would try all through my childhood to emulate.

~

92. My mother never had a cold and never sat down except to eat or sew.

~

93. From the first time I heard the rhyme "eeny, meeny, miney, moe," it became an essential—if not the prime—(and, Lord help me, permanent) component of my decision-making process.

~

94. For the most part, my mother seemed to be too busy doing things for me to look into my eyes.

~

95. As a special treat, my father would occasionally bring home for me a song sheet, picked up at a subway newsstand, so I could learn the words of all the songs on *Your Hit Parade*. ("You'd be so nice to come home to, so nice by the fire"; "Don't sit under the apple tree with anyone else but me, anyone else but me, anyone else but me"; "You got to ac-cent-chu-ate the positive, e-lim-in-ate the negative, don't mess with Mr. In-between."). His own particular favorites were sentimental old standards like "I'm Always Chasing Rainbows" and "I'm Forever Blowing Bubbles."

~

96. My grandfather told me that when he was offered the choice of Bubba or her sister Annie to marry, he said, "I'll take the fat one."

~

"I'll take the fat one."

97. Every Saturday afternoon my girlfriends and I went to see a double feature (mostly 20th Century–Fox, unfortunately—no perky MGM Judy Garland for our gang), plus cartoon (wincing at the animated atrocities) and Movietone News (bored by the interminable black-and-white war) at the Park Plaza, and it would often happen that a man would sit down next to one of us and proceed to expose himself. We'd nudge each other, get up, change our seats, and not give it another thought. Except if he followed us. But even then, we wouldn't think of reporting him to the matron or an usher as we picked up en masse and once more moved to another row.

~

98. In addition to Danny Kaye, Peter Lawford, Van Johnson, Hedy Lamarr, Jeanne Crain, Joan Crawford, and Joan Leslie, I liked Peggy Ann Garner (especially in *A Tree Grows in Brooklyn,* where I identified with her as a fellow sensitive, sad-eyed child of the slums), Alan Ladd, Anne Revere and

Fay Bainter (mothers who never could have been Axis spies, having sacrificed too many sons in the War), Gene Kelly, Rita Hayworth, John Garfield, Cornel Wilde, Robert Walker (except how could he be married to that chipmunk-cheeked Jennifer Jones?), Guy Madison (solely as a pinup), Rory Calhoun (ditto), and Gail Russell's light green eyes.

99. I liked some stars as much for their voices (deep, resonant, silky, seductive) as for their looks. These included James Mason, Ronald Colman, Glenn Langan (in *Margie*), Joseph Cotten, Gregory Peck, and, in a different way, Dorothy McGuire (especially in *A Tree Grows in Brooklyn,* where I knew that under her hardened exterior she really wanted the best for Francie).

100. I couldn't stand Dorothy Lamour, Betty Grable, Dick Powell, William Powell, Bette Davis (except in *Mr. Skeffington*), Betty Hutton (one of these days she's going to jump right out of her skin), bratty Jane Withers, Fred MacMurray (how did he ever get to be a movie star?), Linda Darnell (too many people called me that), Ida Lupino (how could you like a movie star with the same first name as Margery's bubba?), the Dead End Kids (despite the fact that one of them, I think it was Huntz Hall although it might have been Leo Gorcey, was a fellow alumnus of P.S. 104 and even had been a pupil of the very same Ruth E. Leon I had in the fifth grade), Joan Crawford, Sonja Henie (those skating numbers went on forever), Claudette Colbert and her stupid bangs, and usually Carmen Miranda (she did occasionally win me over with a particularly peppy number).

101. My father's favorite actresses were Joan Blondell and Ann Sothern. He admired their moxie and spunk. (So why did he marry the Jewish Janet Gaynor?)

102. I never went to scary movies (meaning anything beyond Sherlock Holmes, Charlie Chan, or *Abbott and Costello Meet Frankenstein*), I never listened to *Inner Sanctum* (the squeaking-door opening was enough to send me scurrying) or rode on a roller-coaster or Ferris wheel (even the merry-go-round made me muzzy).

~

103. For my tenth birthday, Margery (Rose) gave me a book called *They All Are Jews* (Spinoza? Disraeli? Bizet? Francis Salvador, Indian Fighter?), in an effort, I suppose, to awaken some ethnic/religious passion—or, at least, identification in me, something that was lacking in both my parents.

~

104. My mother's idea of a nice after-school snack was a slice of nice warm, seeded rye bread fresh from the M & M Bakery on the Avenue, piled high with some nice sauerkraut trawled from the big wooden barrel at Olinsky's appetizing store.

~

105. My father and I had secret signals under the kitchen table: knock, knock, shake hands. Always done when Her back was turned.

~

106. I once sent anonymous poems on penny postcards to almost every kid in my class, spelling out in rhyme what I considered to be their most egregious fault (e.g., Donald Bloom: B.O. "Donald, there's something I think you should know . . ."). But I foolishly neglected to send one to myself (would its theme have been for some reason you think you are in a position to judge everyone else, perhaps?) so that I wouldn't be considered a prime suspect in this crime of effrontery.

~

107. Every Wednesday, when my mother went to perform her patriotic volunteer duty at a day-care center for kids whose Rosie-the-Riveter mothers were doing war work, I went to Aunt Pearl's for lunch. This meant that I didn't have to make the long icy or blustery or sweltering trek down Brandt Place, and then Nelson Avenue all the way past Featherbed Lane to Shakespeare Avenue. Aunt Pearl was fortunate enough to live right on Featherbed Lane with Uncle Herbie and her two little boys, and every week she served me spaghetti that didn't come out of a can. (My father frequently reprimanded my mother for letting me eat a dangerously large amount of Franco-American spaghetti.)

~

108. My father only struck me once, probably for some misdemeanor that involved being "fresh" to my mother. He rolled up a copy of the *New York Post*, then told me to turn around and delivered several determined whacks across my tush. I made it a point of honor not to cry.

~

109. When our Girl Scout troop was being organized, my mother was all set to be the leader, but then she got pregnant. Dorothy Pearlman's mother, Eva, stepped in as her replacement for a short time, until she got pregnant too. Finally Ruth Kay (pitted skin and black pompadour) volunteered for the job. Luckily for us, she wasn't even married.

~

110. There was a girl in my Girl Scout troop named Joan who lived down the hill at the corner of Brandt Place and Nelson Avenue and whose father had the same name as mine, Samuel Rosenkrantz. The two major differences were that hers was *Dr.* Samuel Rosenkrantz and that he was blind.

111. One of the things I liked best about being a Girl Scout was going to Rockefeller Center to pick out Girl Scout accessories at the Scout Store—stationery for writing to Abbie Raymundo ("Don't you *ever* get in trouble in school?") and the other, lesser pen pals; skinny green leather wallets, all with the official-looking gold trefoil symbol.

112. My father was known as "The Mayor of 37th Street," according to one of his Fur Buyers' Association cohorts, either Meyer or Mack or Jack or Sam or Ruby or Lou or Irving or Hy—none of whom was a fur buyer.

113. My father called a lot of younger men "Junior."

114. The one piece of advice I got from my grand-mother: Never stay in the tub after the water starts running out, or your dirt will get back on you.

115. Once, after seeing a movie (*The Boy With Green Hair?*) and a stage show ("The Glory of

Easter"?) at the Radio City Music Hall and perhaps shopping for accessories at the Scout Store, we went to eat in a restaurant called Churchill's, where there was a long table of old men eating in tuxedos in the late afternoon. All of a sudden, one of them fell dead into his food and was carried out with a white linen napkin over his face. My friends had a hard time swallowing this story when I related it the next morning.

~

116. In the bathroom of the Schwartz apartment on Macombs Road was a framed, embroidered sampler that read:

> *Don't be nervous,*
> *Don't be rough.*
> *You're our guest*
> *And that's enough,*

which I spent many constipated hours trying to interpret.

~

117. My father never sneezed just once or twice. He always sneezed precisely ten times, loud eruptions that were capable of shaking the kitchen table. At some point during my childhood, I started sneezing ten times too, but mine were softer and closer together. There might be a pause after six or seven, but they always totaled ten in the end.

~

at the center of the (heavily retouched) family

118. My father gave me a penny for every word I could fill in in the Sunday *New York Times* crossword puzzle. Sometimes it added up to as much as a quarter.

~

119. My grandfather's shoe store, which had a giant ENNA JETTICK SHOES sign in front, had on the wall yet another colossal nursery rhyme picture painted by my mother and also had a magical fluoroscope (Foot-O-

Scope) machine that showed you in eerie fluorescent out-
line what all the bones of your feet looked like, a device
which I repeatedly climbed up on and looked into.

120. In addition to my grandfather, my grandmother
and four of their five children worked in the store at var-
ious times (my mother said she was too bashful to ever
dare approach a customer), but it was Eddie and Rebecca
(she dressed in smocks bought by my mother at Klein's)
who made it their permanent careers. Eddie addressed
his father as "Boss" at home as well as in the store, and
the two coworker siblings bickered constantly, ven-
omously, at home as well as in the store, while Zada, the
"Boss," just smiled his benign, smooth-skinned smile.

121. When I walked "upstreet" to Park Street, the
main commercial thoroughfare of Attleboro, with my
uncle Eddie, past the family fruit store of his friend Pete
(Constantine) Peters (destined not to return from the
War) and Aunt Jessie's dry goods store, everyone we
met said "Hi." This was a word I had never encoun-
tered in the Bronx.

122. Every summer Sunday we would all drive out in
Uncle Eddie's Pontiac to the farm Uncle Charlie had
bought (sight unseen) on the outskirts of Attleboro with
the $800 settlement he received from the railroad insur-
ance company after his hand was crushed in a New York

Uncle Charlie and Bluma

City trolley car accident in 1903. Luckily, his wife, Bluma
(wrinkled as a proverbial prune), had something of an
agricultural background. They began their enterprise with
two cows, one of which is said to have died after choking
on an apple. One of their sons, a professor at the
University of Oregon, may or may not have been poi-
soned by his wife when he was 27, dying in the parking lot
of a movie house; another was the owner of the infamous
Russian-movie-playing Stanley Theatre (at which I did *not*
donate my new scarf for the welfare of poor Russian
refugee children as erroneously reported); and a third
became the Education Editor of the *New York Times*. The

large main room of the old farmhouse, with the boys' college diplomas hanging on the wall, was always filled with the starchy, sweet smell of freshly picked corn at the boil.

~

123. On one of my first visits to Uncle Charlie's farm—I must have been only a couple of months old—I rolled off and under the bed and for several increasingly hysterical minutes (such a good, quiet baby), no one could find me.

~

124. My uncle Eddie once took me out for a ride on the open road and shot the speedometer up to 100 miles an hour in his seafoam-green Pontiac, the same one I had gotten carsick all over shortly after he bought it when he was discharged from the army.

~

125. There were only two girls in my class who weren't Jewish: Betty Haen and Jeanette Harris. Jeanette Harris might have been half Jewish.

~

126. Every New Year's Eve the Fur Buyers' Association threw a big overnight party at the Statler Hotel, the men in tuxedos, the women in evening gowns (my mother's usually in powder blue–beaded sheath versions of those I painted in art class), while I spent the night at Aunt Pauline and Uncle Harry's.

my mother always referred to this picture as "three generations"

127. I didn't see much point in connecting the dots because you could almost always figure out what the thing was going to be before you even started.

~

128. The only flowers I knew by name were the rose, the tulip, the daisy, the daffodil, and the dandelion.

~

129. When I was three years and eleven months old, the son of Uncle Charlie who had become Education

Editor of the *New York Times* (diploma on the farmhouse wall) thought I did so well with the little twisted metal puzzles he had in his apartment that I should be tested at the Educational Clinic of CCNY. The report came back in mimeographed blue type: Ruth's comprehension and use of language are those generally associated with children of *very superior* intelligence. Ruth's vocabulary is equal to that of an average 6-year-old child. Ruth's mental age is 5 years 8 months. Ruth ranks in the upper 1% of pupils of her age. But who *was* this Ruth? I didn't know anybody named Ruth except for a distant cousin on Uncle Charlie's farm.

130. I liked old S. Z. "Cuddles" Sakall (didn't it start off being spelled Szakall?) because his accent was familiarly foreign. It seemed extremely strange to me if someone (especially a grandparent) over the age of seventy spoke English without an accent.

131. Margery came along on almost all our family excursions.

132. Margery's father, Lou, (possibly) a one-time Minor League baseball player and later employee of his father-in-law (Simon Legree)'s waste materials (junk) business, always sat silently at the kitchen table, a glass of beer by his hand, looking down or staring morosely into space, almost as if he were Irish.

⁓

133. When my father switched from Chesterfields to Pall Malls, he seemed to relinquish a certain degree of masculinity.

⁓

134. My father kept promising to teach me how to play pinochle when I became old enough to grasp the complexities of the game, but that day never came.

⁓

135. Except for the few times Uncle Ed drove to fetch us (vomit in the new green Pontiac), my mother and I took the train to Providence, where he met us to complete the trip to Attleboro. The loud, dragon-like blasts of steam from the train on the tracks of Grand Central started the trip off on a note of terror, but then we would settle down to lunch in the dining car (secret table manner signals) or buy a gentile-tasting sandwich of American cheese and butter on white bread, coloring in a Dionne Quints (born two days after me, which almost made us sextuplets) coloring book, looking out the window at the hurricane-devastated landscape and dictating poems about it for my mother to write down.

136. The three of us wrote poems all the time. When we took a long enough subway ride, my father, mother, and I each had a little pad and a pencil. One of us would come up with a topic and we would compete for who could write the best poem. Poems were written for birthdays and other special occasions. By the time I was seven, there was a complete book of my efforts, transcribed in my mother's handwriting. Occasionally there might be censorship of some of my erratically scanned works. For example, one poem (written when I was sick in bed: no excuse) bore the inscription Written for Uncle Ed on his birthday, but was withheld:

> You never spent your birthday
>   like this before,
> This will be a bore.
>   My nose, stumact and chest is sore.
> You're in the army and will never get out,
> That's why I have to kinda shout—
>   *HAPPY BIRTHDAY!*

137. When I was seven and we moved the five blocks from Tremont Avenue to Brandt Place, my mother really went to town, unleashing all her dormant artistic impulses on the decoration of my room. The color scheme was part Merry Christmas (a holiday never acknowledged in the presence of Aunt Pauline), part Italian flag. Red and white peppermint stripes abounded, in one ruffle running around three sides of the window and another on a kelly-green–painted piano stool that stood before a small desk made by Uncle Harry. The four-poster mahogany bed would have met the royal standards of a Princess Margaret Rose, and in front of it was a dark wood chest painted by my mother (freehand, she boasted) with a Pennsylvania Dutch motif in the same shade of kelly green as the stool.

~

138. Howie, the oldest son of the Greenbergs (Apartment 2D), had been declared Missing in Action, but his family never (publicly) acknowledged the possibility that he might be dead. Mrs. Greenberg, although her features displayed a rather simian cast, had produced several attractive children: Doris (who once baby-sat for me and introduced me to the provocative catch in Frank Sinatra's voice when he sang "I've Got a Crush on You"), Stanley (who was two years older than me and sometimes tried to push me up against the wall in the hallway), the silent Shirley, and the bad-tempered baby sister, Billie (Wilma). Since Howie had disappeared before I moved into the building, I had no idea what he looked like.

139. The Shames family (Apartment 2C) had recently arrived in the Bronx from Omaha, Nebraska, and all four of its members, Mr. and Mrs. Shames, Connie, and Michael, bore a distinct dark and lanky resemblance to Abraham Lincoln.

~

140. As the result of his pulling a pot of boiling water down from the stove and onto himself as a child, there was, in the crook of my father's elbow, a flap of skin covering a deep mysterious hollow to which my finger was inextricably drawn.

~

141. Being sick meant staying home from school and lying in bed between freshly laundered white sheets (delivered to the door once a week), a paper bag pinned to the side for my discarded tissues, reading *Modern Screen* or *Photoplay* (the only movie magazines I considered worthy of my attention), or *Nancy and Sluggo*

PHOTOPLAY combined with MOVIE MIRROR 10¢ DECEMBER

LARGEST CIRCULATION OF ANY SCREEN MAGAZINE

Exclusive! — STIRLING HAYDEN TELLS WHY HE QUIT HOLLYWOOD

comics (ditto), while listening to *Our Gal Sunday* ("Can this girl from a mining town in the West find happiness as the wife of a wealthy and titled Englishman?"), *Lorenzo Jones* (". . . and now, smile a while with Lorenzo Jones and his wife Belle"), and *When a Girl Marries* ("Dedicated to everyone who has ever been in love") on the radio.

142. Six days before my eleventh birthday, I suddenly had a baby sister.

143. The few books on our living-room shelf included *The Settlement Cookbook* (Cook liver until dry and flat?), *The Death of Lord Haw-Haw*, *The Romance of Leonardo da Vinci*, *20,000 Guinea Pigs Can't Be Wrong*, and *Is Sex Necessary?*

144. Both Rose Schwartz and Uncle Harry said things in Yiddish they would never have dreamed of saying in English, such as *Kish mir in toches* (Kiss my ass) or *Kak im un* (Shit on him). Uncle Harry also was fond of employing expressions picked up from the radio: *That ain't the way I heerd it*, *T'ain't funny, McGee*, and *That's the $64 question!*

145. When my sister was born, the announcements went out:

(The truth of the matter was that I really wanted a brother.)

~

146. While my mother was in the hospital convalescing after her cesarean section, she wrote me a note (*My Sweet sweet Linda,*) in faint #1 pencil (no #2 around there anywhere?), telling me that the baby was born looking like an Eskimo papoose and with such long hair the nurses had to braid it (*She has broken one record already—she has more hair than any of the 55 babies in the nursery and it is black as coal, her hands and feet are just like little cushions, her nails are long and lovely like yours and she has a double chin like her mommy's already*). She also told me how proud I would be when I wheeled her out in the street, and that (what did this mean?) *if we didn't have such a wonderful doctor we might have lost sweet little Karen and I might have been dreadfully ill,* and that I'd better start scrubbing my hands in preparation for the baby's arrival home. She also wished me luck marching with my troop in the I Am an American Day parade on Sunday.

147. When we went to the World's Fair in Flushing Meadows, I got a souvenir Heinz pickle pin, and, as we were leaving, a drunken man chased my mother around the parking lot and tried to lift up her skirt. (The last part may have been as much a dream as the dumbwaiter may have been.)

148. To camouflage the detestable, watery canned spinach she served far too often, my mother would mix it up with the (lumpy) mashed potatoes that were left after I had consumed the protein portion (flat and dry) of my meal. Then she would dissect this mixture and say, "Here, dear, just eat this half." After I had done so, she would divide the remainder and say, "Here, dear, just eat this half." She repeated this procedure until the plate was clean and I always finished feeling somewhat triumphant (all gone!), but also decidedly duped.

149. When Aunt Pauline's two sons tickled me until I couldn't stop laughing, they actually were under the misapprehension that I was enjoying myself, when, in fact, I detested it. They also forced me to drink some sickly sweet Coca-Cola which bubbled up my nose and which from that day forward never passed through my lips (or nose) again.

150. During the period when Aunt Helen was engaged to Sam Sigel, there was a certain current of electricity running between them that I liked to stand inside of so I could feel it run through me.

~

151. Of course I never learned to swim. It wasn't in my gene pool, so to speak. One after another, the counselors at camp tried and tried to teach me, but as soon as my head went under water, I would sputter and splutter and flounder and founder like a desperate, drunken crab. So they finally gave up and let me lie on the splintery deck reading and rereading my water-spattered copy of *Here We Are*, an anthology of short stories by Dorothy Parker and Ruth Suckow and Marjorie Kinnan Rawlings and Jesse Stuart and Dorothy Canfield Fisher.

152. I believed that God (long white beard) had bestowed the two richest, most beautiful voices in the world on Kate Smith and Eddie Cantor, with Kathryn Grayson a close third.

153. Uncle Harry was afraid to be alone. He refused to stay at home, even with his boys, without Aunt Pauline being there. Even though he jocularly thumbed his nose and stuck out his tongue at the movie camera when my father tried to film him and said *T'ain't funny, McGee* and *Kak im un* and built beautiful dollhouses for every new girl child in the family and went to his haberdashery clerk job every day on the subway and cheerily scoured the pots after every seder, and even though he had a twinkle in his eye and was as dapper as Adolphe Menjou in starched white shirt and bow tie, he was unable to let Aunt Pauline leave him at night even to go across the street to the Park Plaza to see a movie with my mother and Rose Schwartz.

154. These were the "sports" in which I participated: belly-whopping on my sled down the Brandt Place hill (one time my stockinged foot came out of my boot, landing in the snow, and as I pulled it up, cold and dripping wet, I caught sight of Stanley Greenberg

(Apartment 2D) laughing at me); roller skating down the Brandt Place hill (skate key on a string around my neck), never ranging too far from the brick walls of the buildings, occasionally achieving (nirvana) a modicum of soaring speed; playing potsy—the Bronx version of hopscotch—in the alley, trying desperately to balance on one foot; jumping rope (never double-Dutch); croquet on the level playing field of Bubba's backyard with Aunt Beck, Aunt Helen, and Uncle Ed and sometimes Ruth or Bobby Sharkey from down the street; rounds of catch and hit-the-penny with my father on the sidewalk; punch ball (*Watch out for my glasses!*) in the cavernous school gym (one-piece green gym-suit uniform with fabric belt and ballooning bloomers that were always losing their elastic and that you had to take home for your mother to wash and remember to bring back); skee-ball on the Rockaway boardwalk; rowing at Camp Jekoce (*I can't swim!*).

~

155. I didn't understand baseball or football. Neither the rules nor the enthusiasm (weekend games droning on my father's radio).

~

156. I would fervently thank God (long white beard) for making me a girl and not a boy who would have to fight in the army and hide in a foxhole beside other sweaty, scared young men named Tex, Alabam, and (worst of all) Brooklyn.

157. At the Horn & Hardart Automat—as elegant to me as (and far more entertaining than) Toffinetti's or Churchill's (white linen napkin over dead man's face), with its huge stained-glassed window, fruit-carved moldings, grinning plaster gargoyles, white marble tables, gleaming tile floor—I would be given my own pile of nickels to put in the slot next to the little picture window displaying the tempting dishes, wait for the shelf to revolve (occasionally a mysterious hand would be spied replenishing the supply), then lift up the door to redeem my prize. Even the (creamed) spinach was good at the Automat, too good to taint with mashed potatoes, but I usually chose the creamy macaroni and cheese, crusty on top and flecked with red pimento confetti, accompanied by a (for once cold enough) glass of milk that streamed from the mouth of a metallic fish. (If someone tried to remove Uncle Harry's plate before he was finished, he'd always say "What do you think this is? The Automat?")

~

158. When my father's last two stubble-chinned sisters (*please* don't let them kiss me!) finally got married, one chose for her spouse a wisecracking cabdriver named Milton, the other settled on or for her father's brother.

~

159. My second favorite picture book was *Ferdinand the Bull*. Probably because it was a perfect reflection of my philosophy that it was much better to sit still and be passive and let other people do the running around and fighting (thank you again God for making me a girl!).

~

160. Not surprisingly (Who is Ruth? Who is Linda?), I had from early childhood an exaggerated interest in the resonances of names and was grateful to my parents for not having been called Irving or Goldie. And I always knew that no matter how handsome, rich, or loving he might be, I was not going to marry a Melvin, a Milton, or a Myron, a Schatzberg or a Schnitzer.

~

161. My mother disapproved of short men, almost as if their sub-(her) standard stature made them somehow morally inferior. (In fact the two greatest compliments she could pay a male would be to describe him as tall and educated.) My father wasn't tall, but he wasn't short.

~

162. My uncle Al was a lieutenant, junior grade in the navy and his brother Eddie was a corporal in the Fifth Armored Division of the army. Both of them managed to acquire considerable amounts of merchandise while they were overseas in the war, shipping back extensive services of fine Meissen and Dresden china to their Mumma (a lover of antiques). And for me, Al somehow was able to procure an elegant amethyst

Uncle Ed

necklace as well as a full-size, 120-button mother-of-pearl accordion, both of which were as beyond my years as the Pinocchio pull-toy had been behind.

~

163. Uncle Al also brought home with him a (wife #2) British war bride, a tall, elegant blond woman whose real name was Sheila but whom everyone called Nicky—plus a stepson and a daughter born several months less after the marriage than I thought it was supposed to take to have a baby. Two years later, twins followed, a boy and a girl. A reprobate since high school where he had gotten a girl pregnant, Uncle Al threw away his scholarship to the New England Conservatory of Music (saxophone) to marry his first (*shiksa*) wife Mildred/Mickey.

~

164. I once woke up in the middle of the night, got dressed, ate some cereal and milk (one of the first words I learned to read was "liquid" off the milk bottle), and set off for school.

~

165. I thought of shyness as my chronic disease, at the least provocation spreading over my body like a rash, painful and itchy, making me feverish and mute, wrapping itself tight around my throat, making me long for my mother.

~

166. After considerable practice (and some help from Abbie Raymundo) I finally learned to manage a lopsided somersault, but I never succeeded in accomplishing a cartwheel or a handstand.

~

167. When I was about six, my mother took me to a winter matinee performance of the Ballets Russes de Monte Carlo, two balcony seats on the aisle, but as she stood to help me off with my heavy woolen coat, hat, and mittens, she stepped back into the aisle, not realizing that there was a step, and lost her footing and I had to look on in horror as she rolled down the carpeted stairs till she reached the bottom. The most agonizing part of all was that her skirt rolled up as she rolled down, exposing a bit of her slip, girdle, and garter.

~

168. The clothes that my mother didn't get for me at S. Klein on the (Union) Square (buy half a dozen, have Leya-Linda try them on at home after school, return five of them the next day, bring home some more and start the cycle again), she would whip up on the machine herself (heavy on the plaid, pinafores, smocking, and red rickrack), all with the objective of building up enough inventory so that I would hardly ever have to repeat an outfit all term. (What would *they* think if I did?)

~

169. When I asked my mother why her breasts hung down so flat and floppy, like the African ladies in *National Geographic* (she'd flip them up and dust underneath with talcum powder), she told me that when she was a young woman (when I was a girl), she would bind them down in the fashion of the day (weakening the muscles in the process) so she could be a flat-chested flapper (flop, flip, flap) and wear what *they* were wearing.

~

170. When I was around eight, Daddy suddenly stopped kissing Mommy on the cheek when he came home from work at night.

171. My mother and the two women closest to her had no secrets from each other. This included sharing such intimate subjects as one of them punching tiny holes in her husband's rubbers in order to conceive a second child.

~

172. Sometimes Margery and I would get into vicious fights and make scratches deep into each other's arms.

173. My father never quite shut the door all the way when he was sitting on the toilet.

~

174. When we were at Rockaway Beach, I would make an effort to frolic in the ocean like everyone else and did in fact occasionally enjoy it, by myself or holding hands with a grown-up and jumping up and down in rhythm with the waves. But then one day a tidal-size whopper took me by surprise, and I went under, the breath knocked out of me, eyes and ears filled with foamy, green salt water (something like the water served at Passover seders). As soon as I staggered to my feet and was brought back to our bungalow, I felt a piercing pain in both my ears. For some unfathomable reason (I did not, after all, have much of a past record as a liar or malingerer, despite the seductive pleasures of *Modern Screen* and *Lorenzo Jones*), my parents refused to believe me, which filled me with a feeling of outrage and indignity sharper even than the pain in my ears. Finally, Aunt Pauline, whose family was sharing the small bungalow with ours, decreed that a doctor should be called. When this stranger arrived, he took one look inside my ears and said, "I don't know how this child was able to withstand such pain." Ah, the sweet-tasting antitoxin of vindication.

~

175. One night in Rockaway as I was getting ready for bed, my mother looked at me strangely and said come over here. She wasn't looking at my face, she was looking at my behind and she had gone emphatically silent, the way she always did when she felt any degree of disagreeable emotion. There was consternation in her eyes. Turn around, she said at last, peering at something dangling from between the cheeks of my buttocks. Aunt Pauline better take a look at this, she said. Aunt Pauline (sometimes referred to as Dr. K. by my father) came in and the two women had a concerned consultation, during which I heard such unpleasant words as "intestines" uttered. Finally Dr. K. (the wise old aardvark) decreed that I was to be put into a tub of warm water for further examination. As this was accomplished and I sat there for a few minutes, the increasingly uncomfortable object of their intense scrutiny, they both suddenly burst into peals of laughter (tears at the ready for running down their cheeks) as they realized what the cause was. I appeared to have swallowed a piece of the string that was used to tie up the night before's roast beef, and it was now making its exit the only way it could.

176. I always thought our family was slightly out of step because we got *Newsweek* instead of *Time,* the *Saturday Evening Post* instead of *Life*—or even *Look*—and *Coronet* (full-color reproductions of Old Master paintings) and *Pageant* instead of *Reader's Digest.* We also used Mercurochrome while everyone else used iodine to treat their cuts.

~

177. My mother told me that my two best features (in addition to graceful hands and feet, identical to hers) were my perfectly shaped ears and my widow's peak. The latter was high praise indeed, as she considered a widow's peak to be a great asset in a girl, associated as it was with the most highly desirable heart-shaped face.

~

178. I thought that I looked a little like a young Loretta Young (big brown eyes, generous lips, widow's peak), that my father resembled a Semitic Tyrone Power, that my Zada resembled General George C. Marshall, Cousin Bob a young Dennis Morgan, Aunt Beck a nicer Margaret Hamilton, Cousin Red a more refined Marjorie Main, Uncle Harry the aforementioned Adolphe Menjou, Aunt Pauline the aforementioned Maria Ouspenskaya, Cousin Joe (dead at 36!) the afore-mentioned jollier Edward G. Robinson, Uncle Herbie the aforementioned Brian Donlevy, Uncle Sam the aforementioned Danny Kaye, and my mother every madonna in every old (*Coronet* magazine) Italian Renaissance painting.

179. No one in my family took showers. It seemed, somehow, an overly efficient, gentile thing to do.

~

180. On my grandfather's side ("the *other* side of the family"), there was a contingent of scarcely known cousins living in Pittsburgh, among whom was a doctor named Ben. One afternoon, this Cousin Ben was shot to death in his office by a crazed patient in an exaggerated demonstration of her unrequited love for him.

~

181. My father kept a highly naturalistic yellow ochre plaster dog turd (known in our family as #2) in his top (handkerchief) drawer and would take it out occasionally and put it on the living-room rug to shock visiting cousins or Fur Buyer friends who had come over for coffee and coffee cake and a few hands of pinochle. I considered this to be extremely childish, especially since we didn't have a dog.

~

182. I was constantly asking people what their favorite this or thats were and who or what they liked better or best. Like who/what do you like better, your mother or father, your big sister or your little sister, chow mein or shrimp with lobster sauce, blue ink or purple, roller skating or jump rope, a malted or a milk shake, Fred Astaire or Gene Kelly, Vic Damone or Johnny Johnston? And what's your favorite color, your favorite dessert, drink, name, song, movie, book, who's

your favorite actress, actor, singer, teacher? And, more
to the point, who's your best friend, me or her?

⌒

183. At the small branch library that I attended more
religiously than I did the dreary little *shul* next door, I
determined, once I was allowed into the adult section,
that I would read my way through the fiction shelves,
beginning, of course, with the letter "A." Perhaps
because of its location, this little library had a heavy con-
centration of the works of Sholom (*The Old Country*)
Aleichem and Sholem (*East River*) Asch.

⌒

184. Aunt Helen's
electric engagement to
Sam Sigel culminated
in a grand wedding
(not one in a Romanian
restaurant like my par-
ents') at which I was a
four-year-old flower
girl dressed in a white
dotted swiss gown of
my mother's making,
with dark velvet rib-
bon running around
the neck and puffed

sleeves. My partner for the occasion was ring-bearer
Stanley Sigel, a couple of years my senior, and I
thought that since he already had his tux and I had this

beautiful filmy gown, there was no reason why we wouldn't eventually get married ourselves one day. We even had some snapshots taken holding hands. (A year or two later, the dress was pressed into further service when, with the addition of a pair of ruffled pantaloons run up by my mother on the machine—coordinating black velvet ribbon running around the eyelet lace borders—I wore it Scarlett O'Hara–style, complete with long sausage curls, at the Board of Education dramatic festivities celebrating the Sesqui-Centennial of Schools in America.)

185. After Aunt Annie had her stroke, she would peer with frightened eyes around the corner before she entered a room. For some reason she had left her only daughter back in Russia when she came over.

~

186. I once asked my father how to remove the dirt from under my toenails and he looked at me in disgust. You're not supposed to *get* dirt under your toenails, he said.

~

187. Once in a blue moon we took the train ride (not nearly as long as the one to Providence) to visit our (relatively) rich relatives in Poughkeepsie. They lived in a big Tudor house with an upstairs and a downstairs and my cousins (one two years older than me, the other two years younger, all three of us born in the merry month of May) had their own pretty pink rooms with flowered wallpaper and slanty ceilings, and the living room and dining room were filled with delicate antiques. The girls' mother, Cousin Red, had some connection to my grandmother's sixth sister, the one whose name was never spoken.

~

188. My three favorite toys were: Lincoln Logs, a woodburning set, and a printing kit with racks of small rubber letters with which you could write a whole book, the last two of which I liked as much for their pungent aromas as anything else.

189. Even when there wasn't much money, there was enough to pay a *schwarze* to come in once a week to scrub the kitchen and bathroom floors and dust the majolica pitcher and the white bisque lamp that showed a little boy who appeared to have wet his pants—the etched slogan in its base reading "You naughty boy." The only time Aunt Pauline and Rose spoke full-blown Yiddish was when the *schwarze* was there. My mother understood the language but she didn't speak it.

190. My little sister had glossy dark brown hair and enormous round brown eyes (much bigger than mine) fringed with lush, llama-like black lashes (no retouching needed on her photos) and she stared up at the big Wee Willie Winkie (walking through town in his nightgown) painting on the wall as she lay in her crib drinking milk from a bottle that was cocooned in a blue beanbag-style holder. She was pretty and peppy and (to me) the strangest thing about her was that she gave no indication of being frightened of the world.

191. The only doll I ever really liked was a big celluloid window display mannequin from Aunt Jessie's store, about as unlifelike as a doll could be: no curly hair to comb, no warm and supple baby-like skin, no bright blue glass eyes that sparkled back at you. I never gave it a name and probably didn't play with it much more than Margery played with Shirley, but I enjoyed it as a kind

the celluloid doll

of silent companion and kept it until the day my baby
sister scrawled all over the top of its head with blue
crayon. I couldn't look at it after that.

~

192. I didn't give it a second thought when I said
"Eeny, meeny, miney, mo, catch a nigger by the toe," or
ate little chocolate people-shaped candies we called nigger babies. It didn't seem to conflict at all with reading
sensitive black books like *The Street* by Ann Petry or
writing compositions on brotherhood and tolerance or
my affection for Smitty the mailman.

~

193. I somehow got the idea that my cousin Manny
was the inventor of Mr. Potato Head.

194. Even when we went to the Bronx Zoo or the Aquarium or the NYU Hall of Fame, my father wore a suit (probably brown) and tie, and usually a hat.

~

195. Everything about me seemed to contain a contradiction of itself. I was pretty (petal face) and I was not (four-eyes, blue glasses), I was smart (Ruth's vocabulary is equal to that of an average six-year-old child) and dumb (8×7? 8×7?), I was sloppy (Why can't you put your things away like Margery?) and orderly (my life is a list), I was nice (I let Sunny Berman walk to school with me) and not so nice (I let Sunny Berman be marked late and didn't try to squeeze her into the on-time line).

~

196. My mother couldn't greet the day without "waiting for her call" and then "putting on her face." Her face consisted of a dusting of Lady Esther powder, some rouge, and a few dabs of subdued orange Tangee lipstick and enough eyebrow pencil to compensate for that of which nature had given her short shrift.

~

197. Every year or two my mother would take me to the Mosart [*sic*] Photography Studios on Fordham Road to have my portrait taken. I would be seated on a high stool—sometimes they'd give me a hard plaster doll to pose with—and would try, in my earliest years, to look

my cutest, and later my most ("A Tree Grows in the Bronx") sensitive. There was also a woman in our own building on Tremont Avenue who was an even better photographer, but she gradually went crazy, making faces at the window, something like Aunt Annie.

~

198. I never once had a snapshot of myself taken with my glasses on.

199. When my sister was born, I felt that my father was now hopelessly outnumbered. And so did he.

~

200. In my mother's box of important papers (not to be confused with the Nice Research Work box) she kept a yellowed newspaper clipping showing herself and another woman (girl) named Margaret Wood, under the heading "The Highest Paid Office Workers in New York City." The article went on to explain that this was because they worked for a company (Model Brassiere) that happened to be the topmost tenant in the Empire State Building. My mother, Miss Sillman, gushed, "And the view we get during idle moments (idle? my mother?) is the most entrancing in the whole world, with the entire city spread out before us like an aerial panorama."

~

201. My only household chore was peeling potatoes.

~

202. Every Friday, my father handed over to my mother the small manila envelope that contained his week's pay, taking out a small percentage of it for his own spending money (the Mayor of 37th Street lunched at Dubrow's delicatessen). With this she was supposed to "handle" or "manage" the family finances, but alas, my father felt that it was one of the crosses he had to bear that he had married an irresponsible woman who could neither "handle" nor "manage" money, a subject that he grumbled or bellowed about at the top of his lungs several times a week, prompting me to flee to my room and quietly close the door.

~

203. My mother's idea of cursing was to mutter, "Christopher Columbus!" under her breath. Aunt Beck's was to exclaim, "Canary!"

~

204. There seemed to be a chant for every occasion and activity in my life: tickling (*This little piggy went to market, this little piggy stayed home*), rainy-day doldrums (*Rain, rain, go away, little Leya wants to play*), bad behavior (*but when she was bad she was horrid*), bouncing balls (*A my name is Alice, my husband's name is Al, we come from Arizona and we sell apples*), jumping rope (*I won't go to Macy's any more, more more, there's a big fat policeman at the door, door door, he'll take you by the collar and he'll make you want to holler, so I won't go to Macy's any more, more, more*), responding to an insult (*Sticks and stones will break my bones but names will never harm me*), a walk to Ruschmeyer's on the Avenue for a vanilla cone—Margery liked chocolate—with sprinkles, or to Slater's in Attleboro for homemade pistachio or peach (*I scream, you scream, we all scream for ice cream*), bedtime (*Good night, sleep tight, don't let the bedbugs bite*), petty chicanery (*Made you look, made you look, made you buy a penny book*) and, most glorious of all, the last day of school (*No more pencils, no more books, no more teachers' dirty looks!*).

205. I would try to shock people by telling them my favorite color was black.

~

206. When I couldn't fall asleep at night, I would often try to compose a mental list (my life is a list) of all forty-eight states in alphabetical order . . . Alabama, Arizona, Arkansas, California, Colorado, Connecticut . . . usually becoming frustrated as I struggled to round out the full complement of eight M's, which didn't have such convenient study aids as N did with its (4) New and (2) North states. At other times I tried to think of a child I knew whose name began with every letter of the alphabet. (Thank goodness for Cousin Zelig—who hated his name.) Or else I strained my brain searching for movie stars with double initials: Billie Burke, Claudette Colbert, Dan Dailey, Frances Farmer, Greta Garbo/Greer Garson, Hurd Hatfield, Jennifer Jones (chipmunk cheeks), Lola Lane, Maria Montez, Robert Ryan/Roy Rogers, Simone Simon. (If only I could have looked ahead to Armand Assante, Kevin Kline, Pete Postlethwaite, and Parker Posey.)

~

207. Of course I wasn't totally surprised. I had after all sent away for my copy, in plain brown wrapper, of "Growing Up and Liking It," as advertised in *Calling All Girls* magazine, but seeing that dark red blood seeping through my underpants was still something of a shock. When I called my mother into the bathroom, she immediately produced the sanitary belt and box of

Modess Junior napkins she had at the ready (Nice Research Work). But don't think for one minute, young lady, she said as she fastened the pad to the belt, that I'm going to keep doing this for you for the rest of your life.

AFTERWORD

I was on a plane coming back to Los Angeles from a trip to New York when I opened my notebook and found myself writing the words "500 Things About My Childhood: My Life is [*sic*] a List," followed by a few sentences:

All my elementary school teachers had the same handwriting.

All my aunts floated but none of them swam.

There were only two girls in my class who weren't Jewish.

It was an idea that seemed to have arrived full-blown, complete, out of nowhere, or perhaps out of my deepest subconscious. The rest of the flight found me frantically scribbling a list of words, names, and phrases: Hitler dream, mother's box, dumbwaiter, Francisco Raymundo,

Danny Kaye, Franco-American spaghetti. By the time the plane approached LAX, the notebook was almost filled.

The process of expanding these notes into a book was equally intense, but it moved at a very different pace. It seemed that each item on my life-list, even if it was only a single sentence long, was so loaded that I could process only two or three of them a day. Some, like the idea for the book itself, came fully formed; others required shaping and amplification; some of the longer ones I returned to again and again (pondering over such significant issues as did I really hate Betty Grable or did I just think her nose was too close to her mouth?). I gathered around me all the family photos (of which I have somehow been made the extended family's designated custodian, receiving batches every time someone dies or empties out a basement) I could find, and whatever childhood memorabilia had miraculously been preserved (the report cards, clippings, and letters that had survived my mother's moves and mine), and I found that staring at them would bring me into contact with feelings, experiences, relationships, and people I hadn't thought about since childhood. As a Bronx Realist, I could never say I made a spiritual connection, but these things did form a kind of skeleton key into what I once called (in a poem I wrote when I was thirteen) my memory attic.

As one recollection triggered another, patterns began to form and I could see interconnections (that required the use of a lot of parentheses), memories building upon each other, I saw the symbiotic relationship between Mommy and me in a way I never had quite seen it before, I saw that my early years were a lot more "Jewish" than

I would have thought, and I also saw a little girl who was a network of not always so admirable contradictions. As the book built, piece by piece, I added and subtracted elements until I reached the number that seemed right for me, knowing that when I arrived at the point where my sister was born and I got my period, my childhood was essentially over.

Through all this, the thought struck me several times that in a sense this was an exercise that would be interesting and revealing for other people to try doing, in their own way. It is a process I can heartily recommend.

~